DEVELOPMENT OF
THE UNITED STATES CAPITAL

Courtesy of the United States Army Air Corps

AIRPLANE VIEW OF WASHINGTON, D. C., IN 1929

DEVELOPMENT

OF THE

UNITED STATES CAPITAL

ADDRESSES DELIVERED IN THE AUDITORIUM
OF THE UNITED STATES CHAMBER OF COMMERCE
BUILDING, WASHINGTON, D. C., AT MEETINGS
HELD TO DISCUSS THE DEVELOPMENT
OF THE NATIONAL CAPITAL

APRIL 25-26, 1929

UNITED STATES
GOVERNMENT PRINTING OFFICE
WASHINGTON : 1930

HOUSE CONCURRENT RESOLUTION No. 10

SUBMITTED BY MR. BEERS

Resolved by the House of Representatives (the Senate concurring), That the addresses delivered on April 25 and April 26, 1929, in the auditorium of the United States Chamber of Commerce Building at a meeting held in Washington, District of Columbia, for the purpose of discussing the development of the National Capital, be printed and bound, with illustrations, as a House document, and that six thousand five hundred additional copies be printed, of which four thousand copies shall be for the House, one thousand copies for the Senate, one thousand copies for the Committee on Public Buildings and Grounds of the House, and five hundred copies for the Committee on Public Buildings and Grounds of the Senate.

Adopted December 20, 1929.

For sale by the Superintendent of Documents, Washington, D. C. . . . . Price $1.25 (cloth)

CONTENTS

PROCEEDINGS OF APRIL 25, 1929

PROCEEDINGS OF APRIL 26, 1929

LIST OF ILLUSTRATIONS

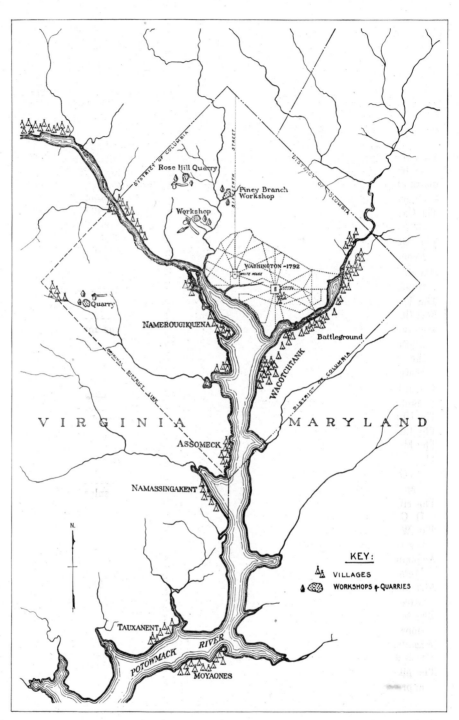

DIAGRAM OF INDIAN VILLAGES

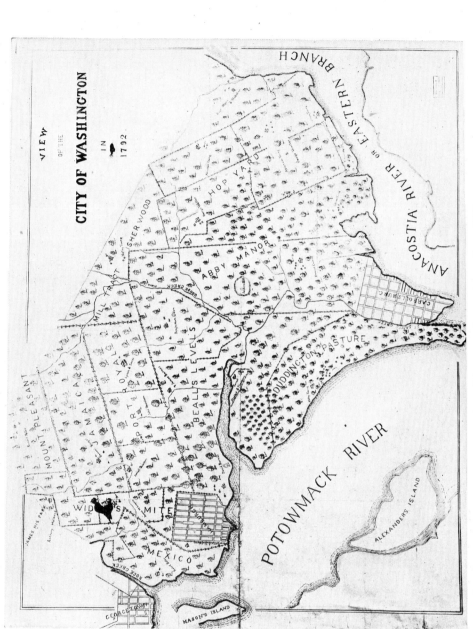

SITE FOR THE "SEAT OF GOVERNMENT" IN 1792

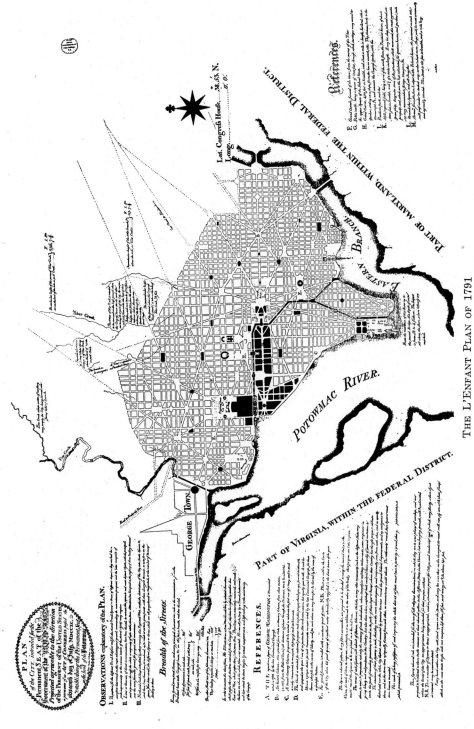

The L'Enfant Plan of 1791

PLAN
of the CITY intended for the
Permanent SEAT of the
Government of the UNITED STATES
Projected agreeable to the direction
of the President of the United States
pursuant to the ACT of Congress passed on
the sixteenth day of July, MDCCXC "establishing the Permanent Seat on the bank of the Potowmac"

OBSERVATIONS explanatory of the PLAN.

I. The positions for the different Grand Edifices and for the several Grand Squares or Areas of different shapes as they are laid down were first determined on the most advantageous ground commanding the most extensive prospects, and the better susceptible of such improvements as the various intents of the several objects may require.

II. Lines or Avenues of direct communication have been devised as connect the separate and most distinct objects with the principal, and to preserve through the whole a reciprocity of sight at the same time. Attention has been paid to the passing of those leading Avenues over the most favorable ground for prospect and convenience.

III. North and South lines, intersected by others running due East and West, make the distribution of the City into Streets, Squares etc., and those lines have been so combined as to meet at certain given points with those divergent Avenues so as to form on the spaces "first determined" the different Squares or Areas, which are all proportional in Magnitude to the number of Avenues leading to them.

Breadth of the Streets.

Every grand transverse Avenue and every principal divergent one, such as the communication from the President's house to the Congress house, etc., are 160 feet in breadth, and thus divided:

10 feet of pavement on each side	20 Feet
30 feet of gravel walk planted with trees on each side	60
80 feet in the middle for carriage way	80
	160

The other streets are of the following dimensions, viz:

Those leading to public buildings or markets	130 Feet
	110-90
Others	110-90

In order to execute the above plan, Mr. Ellicott drew a true Meridional line by celestial observation which passes through the Area intended for the Congress house; this line he crossed by another due East and West, which passes through the same Area. These lines were accurately measured and made the bases on which the whole plan was executed. He ran all the lines by a Transit Instrument and determined the Acute Angles by actual measurement, and left nothing to the uncertainty of the Compass.

REFERENCES.

A. The equestrian figure of George Washington, a Monument voted in 1783 by the late Continental Congress.

B. An historic Column, also intended for a Mile or Itinerary Column, from whose station (a mile from the Federal house), all distances of places through the Continent are to be calculated.

C. A Naval Itinerary Column proposed to be erected to celebrate the first rise of a Navy and to stand a ready Monument to consecrate its progress and Achievements.

D. This Church is intended for National purposes, such as public prayer, thanksgivings funeral Orations, etc., and assigned to the special use of no particular Sect or denomination, but equally open to all. It will be likewise a proper shelter for such monuments as were voted by the late Continental Congress for those heroes who fell in the cause of liberty and for such others as may hereafter be decreed by the voice of a grateful Nation.

E. Five grand fountains intended with a constant spout of water. N. B. There are within the limits of the City about 25 good springs of excellent water abundantly supplied in the driest season of the year.

The Squares coloured yellow, being fifteen in number, are proposed to be divided among the several States in the Union for each of them to improve, or subscribe a sum additional to the value of the land for that purpose, and the improvements round the Squares to be completed in a limited time.

The center of each Square will admit of Statues, Columns, obelisks, or any other ornaments, such as the different States may choose to erect, to perpetuate not only the memory of such individuals whose Counsels or military achievements were conspicuous in giving liberty and independence to this Country, but also those whose usefulness hath rendered them worthy of general imitation; to invite the youth of succeeding generations to tread in the paths of those Sages or heroes whom their Country has thought proper to celebrate.

The situation of these Squares is such that they are the most advantageously and reciprocally seen from each other, and as equally distributed over the whole City district, and connected by spacious Avenues round the grand Federal improvements, and as contiguous to them, and at the same time as equally distant from each other, as circumstances would admit. The settlements round those Squares must soon become connected.

This mode of taking possession of, and improving the whole District at first must leave to posterity a grand idea of the patriotic interest which promoted it.

These figures coloured red, are intended for use of all religious denominations, on which they are to erect places of worship, and are proposed to be allotted to them in the manner as those coloured yellow to the different States in the Union; but no burying grounds will be admitted within the limits of the City, an appropriation being intended for that purpose without. N. B. Then a number of Squares or Areas unappropriated, and in situations proper for Colleges and Academies, and of which every Society whose object is national may be accommodated. Every house within the City will stand square on the Streets, and every lot, even those on the divergent Avenues, will run Square with their fronts, which on the most acute angle will not measure less than 56 feet and many will be above 110 feet.

Pine Creek, whose water, if necessary, may supply the City, being turned into James White's branch

	F. I. Pts.
Perpendicular height of the source of Tiber Creek, above the level of the tide in said Creek.	236 "7'5/8

Perpendicular height of James White's Spring being part of Tiber Creek above the level of the tide in said Creek.

This branch of the Tiber, is intended to be conveyed to the President's house.

The water of this Creek is intended to be conveyed on the high ground, where the Congress house stands, and after watering that part of the city, its overplus will fall from under the base of that Edifice, and in a Cascade of 20 feet in height, and 50 in breadth into the reservoir below; thence to run in three fills through the Garden into the grand Canal.

The perpendicular height of the ground where the Congress house stands, is above the tide of Tiber Creek, 78 feet.

Lat. Congreſs Houſe,.. 38.. 53. N.
Long. .... 0.. 0′.

References.

F. Grand Cascade, formed of the Water from the sources of the Tiber.

G. Public walk, being a square of 1,200 feet, through which carriages may ascend to the upper Square of the Federal house.

H. Grand Avenue, 400 feet in breadth, and about a mile in length, bordered with gardens, ending in a slope from the houses on each side. This avenue leads to the Monument A, and connects the Congress Garden with the President's park, and the

I. Well improved field, being a part of the walk from the President's house, of about 1,800 feet in breadth, and ¾ of a mile in length. Every lot, deep coloured red, with green plots, designates some of the situations which command the most agreeable prospects, and which are the best calculated for spacious houses and gardens, such as may accommodate foreign Ministers, etc.

L. Around this Square, and all along the

M. Avenue from the two bridges to the Federal house, the pavement on each side will pass under an Arched way, under whose cover Shops will be most conveniently and agreeably situated. This street is 160 feet in breadth, and a mile long.

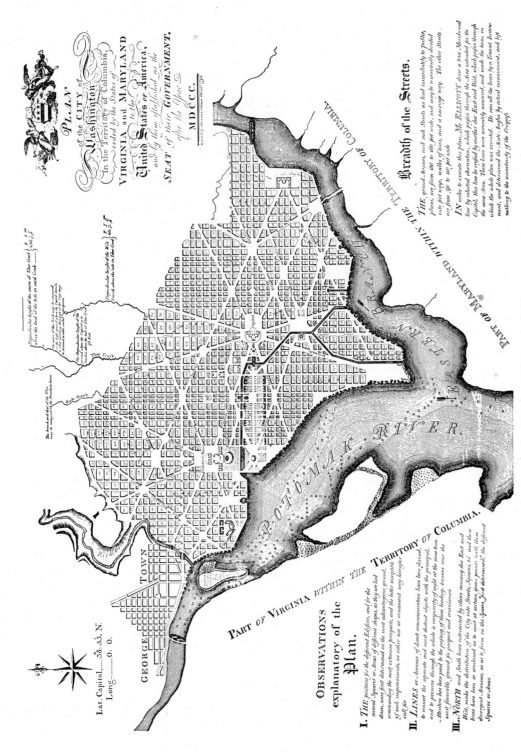

THE ELLICOTT PLAN OF 1792

PLAN of the CITY of Washington in the Territory of Columbia ceded by the States of VIRGINIA and MARYLAND to the United States of America, and by them established as the SEAT of their GOVERNMENT, after the Year MDCCC.

Lat Capitol____38.53. N.
Long_____0: 0.

Perpendicular height of the source of Tiber Creek above the level of the tide in said Creek_____ F. I. Pts. 236.7.5/8

This branch and that of the Tiber may be conveyed to the President's house.

The water of this Creek may be conveyed on the high ground where the Capitol stands, and after watering that part of the City, may be destined to other useful purposes.

The perpendicular height of the ground where the Capitol is to stand, is above the tide of Tiber Creek 78 Feet.

Perpendicular height of the West branch above the tide in Tiber Creek_____ F. I. Pts. 115.7.2/8

OBSERVATIONS explanatory of the Plan.

I. The positions for the different Edifices, and for the several Squares or Areas of different shapes, as they are laid down, were first determined on the most advantageous ground, commanding the most extensive prospects, and the better susceptible of such improvements, as either use or ornament may hereafter call for.

II. Lines or Avenues of direct communication have been devised to connect the separate and most distant objects with the principal, and to preserve through the whole a reciprocity of sight at the same time. Attention has been paid to the passing of those leading Avenues over the most favorable ground for prospect and convenience.

III. North and South lines intersected by others running due East and West, make the distribution of the City into Streets, Squares, &c.; and those lines have been so combined as to meet at certain given points with those divergent Avenues, so as to form on the Spaces "first determined," the different Squares or Areas

Breadth of the Streets.

The grand Avenues, and such Streets as lead immediately to public places are from 130 to 160 feet wide, and may be conveniently divided into foot ways, walks of trees, and a carriage way. The other streets are from 90 to 110 feet wide.

In order to execute this plan, Mr. Ellicott drew a true Meridional line by celestial observation, which passes through the Area intended for the Capitol; this line he crossed by another due East and West which passes through the same Area. These lines were accurately measured, and made the basis on which the whole plan was executed. He ran all the lines by a Transit Instrument, and determined the Acute Angles by actual measurement, and left nothing to the uncertainty of the Compass.

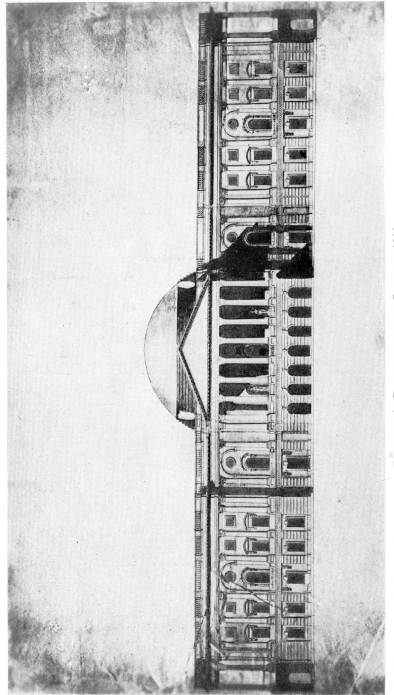

THORNTON'S DESIGN FOR THE CAPITOL, 1800

PROCEEDINGS OF APRIL 25, 1929

VIEW OF THE CAPITOL AFTER ITS DESTRUCTION BY FIRE IN 1814

THE REMAKING OF THE NATIONAL CAPITAL

ADDRESS OF

ANDREW W. MELLON

Secretary of the United States Treasury

TO-NIGHT history repeats itself. We are met under circumstances almost identical with those under which a meeting was held 25 years ago in the old Arlington Hotel, only a short distance from this place. Then, as now, it was a meeting of those representing the Government, and it was held for the purpose of considering plans to make more beautiful the city of Washington.

The principal speaker on that occasion was President Roosevelt. The Congress of the United States was represented by the speeches of Speaker Cannon and others; and Mr. Root, with his great eloquence, championed the cause which he had so much at heart and which he, himself, had done so much to advance.

On that historic occasion the host was the American Institute of Architects. It is most fitting, therefore, that to-night we should have as our guests the representatives of that great and influential organization, to whose foresight and untiring efforts we owe not only the revival but the preservation and advancement of a plan for the orderly and systematic development of the Nation's Capital.

The meeting held in 1905 centered attention on the needs of Washington. At the same time it made certain that the future development of the city should conform to a balanced and comprehensive plan, based upon the spacious and dignified ideas of President Washington and Major L'Enfant, with such modifications as might be required to meet modern conditions and the city's growth.

Now we are engaged in trying to carry out those ideas. Conditions have reached a stage where economy demands that the Government's activity should be adequately housed in buildings owned by the Government itself; and, in order to meet this need, Congress has made the necessary appropriations to begin this work and to proceed with certain other plans for the orderly development of the city. The responsibility for the condemnation and purchase of sites and the erection of most of these buildings has been placed by Congress on the Treasury Department and has become, therefore, an integral part of Treasury activities.

The placing of these buildings involves a great responsibility, for the proper determination of this question will largely influence the future development of Washington. Before coming to a decision the Treasury obtained the advice of Mr. Edward H. Bennett, of Chicago, a well-known architect, whose efforts have had so much to do with bringing to completion the plans for beautifying his native city. Mr. Bennett was appointed Consulting Architect of the Treasury; and, with a small group of other eminent architects from different parts of the country, has given unstintedly of his services in arriving at a solution of this problem.

These men have come to Washington at frequent intervals and have served without adequate remuneration in helping to work out a plan under which the new buildings shall be grouped and designed in such a way as to contribute in the greatest measure possible to the beauty of Washington. In evolving these plans the Treasury has had the cooperation of the Fine Arts Commission and its able and devoted chairman, Mr. Moore; with the Capital Park and Planning Commission; the Office of Public Buildings and Parks; and especially with those Members of the Senate and House of Representatives who are most directly concerned in this work and who have been so largely responsible for the developments now under way.

All of these developments have been embodied in a comprehensive plan, and it is this plan which will be presented to you to-night. We want also to have you view the model which has been made of public buildings to be erected along Pennsylvania Avenue. This model is on view to-night in a room adjoining the one in which we are now and will be taken later to the Treasury, where it will be left permanently on exhibition for all who care to view it.

It was to place these plans before you and also to make something in the nature of a visual presentation through motion pictures that have been prepared that we have asked this distinguished audience to come together to-night. I hope that the plans will meet with your approval so that we can proceed with carrying them out, fortified in the knowledge that we have your sanction and support. I am sure in advance of your deep interest, for it is a work which makes a strong appeal to everyone and gives us all an opportunity to do something of permanent value for the country.

No one has taken a deeper interest in this great undertaking than has President Hoover. In all the things that have been done and are now under way he has given his counsel and support, and behind the plans which have been made for the future he has placed the full force of his administration. It is a great privilege to have him here to-night and to have the honor of announcing the President of the United States, who will now address you.

VIEW OF THE PRESIDENT'S HOUSE AFTER ITS DESTRUCTION BY FIRE IN 1814

(The building is in the background)

SOUTH FRONT OF THE PRESIDENT'S HOUSE IN 1824

WASHINGTON, THE CITY BEAUTIFUL

ADDRESS OF

HERBERT HOOVER

President of the United States

AM GLAD that the opportunity has come to me as President to contribute to impulse and leadership in the improvement of the National Capital. This is more than merely the making of a beautiful city. Washington is not only the Nation's Capital; it is the symbol of America. By its dignity and architectural inspiration we stimulate pride in our country, we encourage that elevation of thought and character which comes from great architecture. Our Government in Washington has grown greatly during the past 15 years. We have a working force of nearly 70,000 employees as compared with 35,000 a score of years ago.

War and economic recovery have delayed us in providing even our bare necessities of office space. Nearly 25,000 employees are to-day in rented buildings or temporary structures built during the war, which were expected to last but a year or two. Many of the buildings are insanitary. Above all, the departments are divided among scores of unworkable and scattered buildings. For instance, Agriculture is housed in 46 different places in the city and the Treasury in 27 places; Commerce in 20 places. We are paying rents and losing efficiency in sums far greater than the interest upon adequate buildings. Many of the buildings we occupy are an eyesore to the city. We have an authorized building program for, say, 18,000 employees, yet if we would satisfy even our present need we should have new buildings to accommodate more than 30,000 Government workers.

Congress has authorized the beginning of a great program which must extend over many years. It is our primary duty to do more than erect offices. We must fit that program into the traditions and the symbolism of the Capital. Our forefathers had a great vision of the Capital for America, unique from its birth in its inspired conception, flexibility, and wonderful beauty. No one in 150 years has been able to improve upon it.

The founders of the Republic also gave us a great tradition in architecture. In after years we have held to it in some periods and in others we have fallen sadly away from it. Although it is, perhaps, too early to envisage such a glorious future, I do hope to live to see the day when we shall remove from Washington the evidences of those falls from the high standards which would have been deplored by the founders of our Republic and have been deplored by the citizens of good taste ever since these transgressions.

Probably one of the major buildings which we regret most is the State, War, and Navy Building. I have been vastly interested to find that the Congress of that day had a splendid taste, for they directed it to be the duplicate of the Treasury Building, but the administration of that day delivered it externally over to an architectural orgy. I have been lately advised that for a comparatively modest sum we can strip it of its function to represent the different types of architecture known to man and bring it back to the sound classic lines of the Treasury, as Congress intended. And this again points to the responsibility of the administration, for Congress is to-day, as then, giving generous authority and asking that we do our part in design and construction.

It is the wish and the demand of the American people that our new buildings shall comport with the dignity of the Capital of America, that they shall meet modern requirements of utility, that they shall fulfill the standards of taste, that they shall be a lasting inspiration. In architecture it is the spiritual impulse that counts. These buildings should express the ideals and standards of our times; they will be the measure of our skill and taste by which we will be judged by our children's children.

Mr. Mellon has insisted that the great responsibility before us is not one which can be discharged by any one individual. It must be the product of the common mind of many men, devout to secure for America the vast realization of the expression of our Nation. And I am confident that we have within the Nation the taste, skill, and artistic sense to perform our task, for our architects have already given to America the leading place in their great art.

It is on this national stage that the great drama of our political life has been played. Here were fought the political battles that tested the foundations of our Government. We face similar problems of our time, and here centuries hence some other Americans will face the great problems of their time. For our tasks and their tasks there is need of a daily inspiration of surroundings that suggest not only the traditions of the past but the greatness of the future.

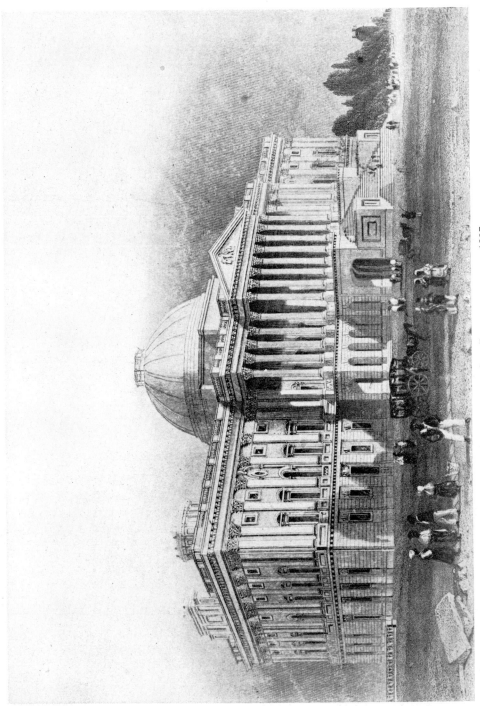

The Capitol Upon Its Restoration in 1827

Original water color by C. Burton, 1824   The Capitol from Pennsylvania Avenue in 1830

22

APPROPRIATIONS FOR PUBLIC BUILDINGS

ADDRESS OF

REED SMOOT

United States Senator, and Chairman Public Buildings Commission

HE President has told you of the great importance of the work on which we are engaged in building a beautiful capital city. Now, I want, in a very few words, to tell you of the ways and means by which we hope to accomplish it.

For a quarter of a century I have had a desire and unfailing faith that I would see Washington, America's Capital City, the most beautiful city in the world. The realization of this desire and faith is near at hand. I call to mind that the late Senator Heyburn and myself, 21 years ago, thought the time had arrived to purchase the privately owned land in the triangle and had in mind the beginning of the erection of buildings to supply the needs of the Government, thus making it the center of the Nation's activities. Senator Heyburn exhibited drawings of a type of building he thought ought to be approved.

An appropriation of $10,000,000 was asked for the purchase of the land. This vast sum asked for at that time was the death knell of the plan. For one, I am thankful it failed, for if it had succeeded we would never have had anything to compare with the plans now fully under way. A twenty-million appropriation in 1908 is fairly comparable with two hundred millions to-day, the amount that will be required to complete the present triangle building program.

Congress has already authorized $75,000,000 for public buildings in the District of Columbia. Of this amount $50,000,000 is to be used for construction of buildings and $25,000,000 for the acquisition of land on which these buildings are to be erected. Most of this latter sum will be spent in acquiring land in the so-called triangle area, extending along Pennsylvania Avenue from Fifteenth Street to the Capitol and bounded on the south side by the Mall. The former sum of $50,000,000 will include a site which has already been purchased for the Supreme Court Building, facing the Capitol and extending along East Capitol Street, covering an area approximating that of the Congressional Library on the south side of the street. A commission, of which the Chief Justice is chairman, is now securing a design for the building.

As regards acquiring sites, there are 23 city blocks involved; and of this number 4 have been purchased, 9 are now in process of condemnation, and condemnation proceedings will be started for 6 within the next month. This leaves only 4 blocks yet to be appropriated for, and it is expected that shortly after the next regular session of Congress convenes an appropriation will be made to complete the purchase of the land in question.

Now, for the buildings: Under the $50,000,000 authorization, $43,500,000 will be expended for construction, the balance to be expended for sites for certain of these projects. Some of this work is now under way. An administration building connecting the two existing wings of the Department of Agriculture is being built at a cost of $2,000,000. The Agricultural Department will also have another building to be constructed shortly on the south side of the administration building, containing a number of laboratories and housing many activities now scattered in other buildings.

An extension to the Government Printing Office will be made at a cost of $1,250,000. A beautiful building for the Bureau of Internal Revenue is being built at a cost of $10,000,000. This building will be a part of the triangle development and will cover the area bounded by Tenth, Twelfth, B, and C Streets NW. It is expected that this building will be completed in a little over two years. It will house all the activities of the Internal Revenue Bureau, now so widely scattered throughout the city.

A building for the Department of Commerce is being erected at a cost of $17,500,000. It is the largest building that will be constructed in the triangle area and will be over 1,000 feet in length along Fifteenth Street, and will extend from the Mall to Pennsylvania Avenue and Fourteenth Street.

An archives building has been authorized at a limit of cost of $8,750,000. This will be one of the most important buildings in the triangle group. It will house the archives and valuable records of the Government, which are now scattered in many buildings, some of which are not fireproof.

Designs are being made for other buildings in the triangle group for the Departments of Justice and Labor and the Interstate Commerce Commission and other independent establishments, as you will see by a model of these buildings on view in the adjoining room. When finally completed the triangle area will contain a most magnificent group of buildings. These buildings, by grouping together related governmental activities, will greatly add to the convenience of those doing business with the Government. They will also make it possible to operate the Government more efficiently and, in the end, more economically by putting an end to the large rent bill which the Government is now paying for offices to house the Departments of Justice, Labor, Commerce, and others.

In addition to the triangle project it is expected that additional accommodations will be provided for the legislative branch of the Government by constructing an addition to the House Office Building on the south side of the Capitol at an estimated cost of $7,500,000, and by enlarging the Senate Office Building, thus completing the quadrangle of which the present building forms three sides, the cost of which is not established, but will probably be somewhat over $2,000,000.

An appropriation of $4,912,414 has been authorized for completing the park between the Capitol and the Union Station and also carrying out the long-delayed plans for the development of the Mall. At the western end of the Mall the Arlington Memorial Bridge is now under way, and when finally completed will represent a total cost of $14,750,000. This will include, besides the bridge, the construction of a plaza west of the Lincoln Memorial, the improvement of Columbia Island in the Potomac, a formal terraced avenue on the Virginia side leading to Arlington Cemetery, and the widening of several streets in Washington to give suitable approach to the bridge.

All of these plans, when carried out, will add greatly to the convenience and beauty of the city. They will not involve a very great outlay each year. For the great triangle development it has been estimated that only $11,000,000 will be expended this year and next year only $24,000,000.

The plans have been carefully made and will, I believe, meet general approval. I am a strong believer in the necessity of carrying forward this great work in an orderly and systematic manner, and am confident that in so doing we will merit the thanks and approbation of future generations who will come here to view the work which we have done.

THE NORTH FRONT OF THE PRESIDENT'S HOUSE IN 1829

The Treasury Building in 1855

FORT STEVENS IN 1864

FORT STEVENS, DISTRICT OF COLUMBIA

(This monument marks the spot where President Lincoln viewed the battle)

(View looking northwest)

THE UNFINISHED WASHINGTON MONUMENT IN 1867

CONGRESS AND THE NATION'S CAPITAL

ADDRESS OF

RICHARD N. ELLIOTT

Member of Congress, and Chairman House Committee on Public Buildings and Grounds

WASHINGTON, the Capital of the United States, is the only city in the country that is purely Federal in its character. It is governed by the President and the Congress, the citizens having no voice in its government. It is what our forefathers intended it to be, the home of our Federal Government, and Congress should make it a model city, the greatest Capital in the world.

Congress, meeting in Philadelphia in 1790, passed an act removing the Capital from that city to the District of Columbia, a tract of land containing 100 square miles of territory which was ceded to the Federal Government by the States of Maryland and Virginia. It was located at the head of tidewater on the Potomac River as a compromise between the representatives of the thirteen original States. This was the first act of Congress relating to the Capital in its present location. The city was laid out by Maj. Pierre Charles L'Enfant, a French Army engineer, in accordance with the act of Congress and under the supervision and direction of President George Washington. The plat of the city could well be used by any great city planner of to-day and reflects great credit upon its authors. It was planned to facilitate the movement of troops through the city, and its broad avenues extend in every direction, making all parts of the city easy of access from any given point.

While in 1790 the greed of man had not yet been felt in the destruction of nature's great forests and natural parks, which God designed and created for the welfare, pleasure, and happiness of the people, the planners of the Capital realized that some day there would be great need in this city for parks and breathing places for its inhabitants. They provided the Mall and other parks which form the nucleus of the beautiful park system in the National Capital, of which we all are justly proud.

The first buildings authorized by Congress were the Capitol, White House, and Land Office. After the partial destruction of the Capitol and the White House by the British Army in 1814 these buildings were rebuilt and the Capitol enlarged and extended. The Capitol and the White House have been enlarged from time to time under various acts of Congress, and the Capitol assumed its present form shortly before the Civil War, when the House and Senate wings were built under the supervision of Jefferson Davis, who was then Secretary of War.

Since 1790 Congress has passed various laws providing for the erection of buildings and other improvements in the Capital, and many plans were suggested and adopted for its improvement and beautification, but no great forward step was taken in the rebuilding of the National Capital until Congress passed the public building law of May 25, 1926, which authorized the construction of public buildings in the District of Columbia to the amount of $50,000,000.

This law was quickly followed by the triangle bill, which authorized the purchase of all the land bounded by Pennsylvania Avenue, Third Street, Missouri Avenue, B Street, and Fifteenth Street NW. The land is to be cleared of buildings and used for the sites for the magnificent public buildings shown on the model exhibited here to-night. They will be easy of access to the people who have business to contract with the Government, a matter that will be highly appreciated by all who have experienced the difficulty we have had to contend with in the widely scattered bureaus and departments as they are now located. For instance, the Department of Agriculture has been occupying space in 47 different and widely scattered rented buildings in the District of Columbia; the Bureau of Internal Revenue has occupied space in 19 buildings; and all departments of the Government have been likewise congested. In addition to this, the archives of the Government, many of them priceless, many of them records on which our glorious history rests, containing the records of the World War soldiers, have of necessity been kept in nonfireproof buildings where they have been under grave danger of destruction for many years. Some of the buildings authorized under the terms of the public building law of 1926 are for the Departments of Commerce, Agriculture, Labor, Justice, Bureau of Internal Revenue, Archives Building, and additions to the Government Printing Office and the Bureau of Engraving and Printing. The passage of this act marked an epoch in the history of the public buildings of our country for the reason that it was the beginning of the first comprehensive building program adopted by our Government. It not only took into consideration the need for public buildings in the District of Columbia but provided for much-needed public buildings throughout continental United States and its dependencies. The Sixty-ninth and Seventieth Congresses will go down in history as doing more in a constructive way for the remaking of the National Capital and the providing of adequate public buildings throughout the country than all the preceding Congresses had done in this behalf.

ADDRESS OF RICHARD N. ELLIOTT

Our Government under the Constitution is divided into three great departments—the legislative, executive, and judicial. The Supreme Court has never had a satisfactory or adequate home. After the Senate wing of the Capitol was built just before the Civil War the old Senate Chamber was turned over to this great court for a court room, and it has held its sessions in that chamber since that time. It is without doubt the greatest court in the world. Its decisions are felt and respected by all our people, most of whom will be surprised to know that the average county-seat court in the United States is better housed than is the Supreme Court. Under the terms of the public building act a new Supreme Court House will be erected on the block of ground north of the Congressional Library which will be in keeping with its dignity and importance.

Another important act passed by Congress was the authorization of the Arlington Memorial Bridge, which was the dream of Andrew Jackson, President of the United States, who insisted that there should be a bridge of enduring granite spanning the broad bosom of the Potomac as a symbol of the union of the North and the South. Within a short time that dream will be realized in the completion of the great bridge now under construction; and it is a coincidence that the construction work of this great bridge has been done under the supervision of Lieut. Col. U. S. Grant, 3d, a grandson of the late Gen. U. S. Grant. A magnificent boulevard has been authorized connecting the west end of the Arlington Bridge with Mount Vernon, the home of Washington. B Street is to be widened to the width of 120 feet from the Senate Office Building to the Potomac River. Twenty-third Street NW. will be widened as far north as Washington Circle. B Street between the Government buildings and the Mall will be the great thoroughfare over which processions going from the National Capitol to Arlington Cemetery will travel.

Last, but not least, is the act of March 4, 1929, a bill for the enlarging of the Capitol Grounds. It authorizes the opening of a boulevard from the Columbus Monument, in front of the Union Station, to a point where it will intersect with Pennsylvania Avenue at Second Street, and it provides for the extension of the Capitol Park to the Union Station, and removes all the old buildings therefrom. It is said that the signing of the bill was the last official act of President Calvin Coolidge, who was a great friend of all the legislation seeking to improve and rebuild the National Capital. His administration will go down in history as marking the beginning of the great reconstructive period in the National Capital. The work of constructing these great buildings is placed by law in the hands of the Secretary of the Treasury. Secretary Mellon and his able corps of assistants have been working hard to carry on this great work and complete it at the earliest possible time, and they deserve great praise and credit for the start they have made in carrying out the mandate of

Congress. It is well to note that in this time of reconstruction of the National Capital we are fortunate in having as Chief Executive of the Nation a man who is a trained engineer and builder, one whose life has been devoted to the handling of large affairs. President Hoover by reason of his great ability and industry will have many constructive achievements to his credit at the end of his administration, and he will no doubt go down in history as the great builder, and the monument to his administration will be Washington, the finest capital in the world.

The United States Soldiers' Home in 1870

THE LIBRARY OF CONGRESS AS COMPLETED IN 1897

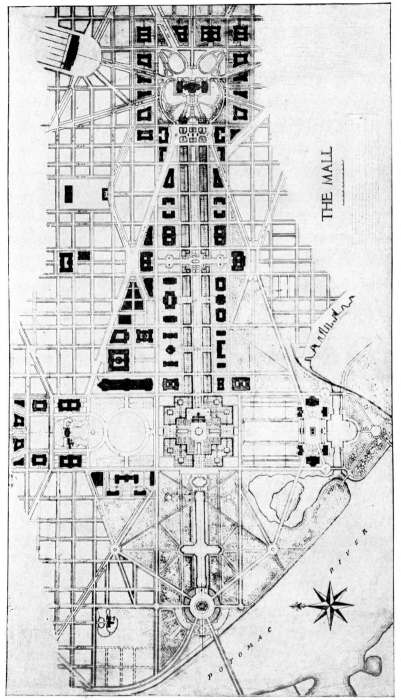

THE MALL

THE McMILLAN PLAN OF 1901, SHOWING THE MALL

The McMillan Commission of 1901 prepared a plan providing for a return to the spirit of the original L'Enfant plan, including a great avenue from the Capitol to the Washington Monument. The plan also recommended the Lincoln Memorial and the Arlington Memorial Bridge, and the removal of the railroad tracks from the Mall. The new Union Station, the Lincoln Memorial, and a large number of other buildings in the area have been located in general accordance with this plan.

THE UNION STATION IN 1910 AS DEVELOPED UNDER THE McMILLAN PLAN

MAKING A CAPITAL CITY

ADDRESS OF

MILTON B. MEDARY

Member of the National Capital Park and Planning Commission

THE physical plan of a city should bear the same relation to the development of its separate elements that a constitution or charter bears to the development of the social and political life of its people. Washington and his advisers recognized this fact and gave us a physical plan with our Constitution. Had they anticipated the chaos and anarchy associated with the physical development of many American cities during the period which followed the early Republic, I am inclined to think they would have provided a Government agency as guardian of the physical plan of Washington in much the same manner as the Supreme Court is called upon to measure the development of social and political institutions in terms of the Constitution.

Such a plan must necessarily be basic and flexible enough to permit the freest development in accordance with the varying conditions of a constantly changing social order, insisting only that all individual elements of a city's growth shall be in harmony with each other and with the whole.

The value of large and farseeing planning is by no means confined to the æsthetic. In considering each project in the development of a city as a part of a grand purpose great economies result from the avoidance of overlapping interests and the consequent destruction of previous development by the encroachment of newer work and through the conveniences of use resulting from orderly arrangement of related interests. Each step in such a program gradually but consistently leads in the direction of that true simplicity in the arrangement of the city as a whole which can result only from a singleness of purpose behind all of its physical works.

Without such purpose physical chaos will eventually deprive a city of much of its usefulness as well as its dignity. The period of artistic illiteracy which governed the development of Washington during the period between the influence of the L'Enfant plan and the plan of 1901 well illustrates this point, a notable example being the introduction of railroad tracks and stations in the great park designed by

L'Enfant and known as the Mall. The cost and manner of correcting this mistake illustrate both the lack of economy resulting from unguided development and the value to a city of the orderly disposition of its utilities in their true relation to a great basic plan. The great industries of the country never hesitate to scrap entire plants if badly planned, not for æsthetic reasons but as a necessary measure of economy of production and maintenance, and our universities, hospitals, and other large institutions are frequently under the same necessity.

Huge as our country has become, and accustomed as we are to large figures, we are often staggered by large plans because of the ultimate cost of their realization. The size and cost of the ultimate realization of the city of Washington as planned by L'Enfant did not seem extravagant to Washington and the group of his advisers who dictated that plan. The infant Republic was in no position to think of its immediate realization, but nevertheless it was planned to be the capital of what Washington believed would be a great nation, and in discussing such details of the plan as the size of the White House he stated that the plans were being made for a far-distant future.

The McMillan plan, made in 1900, is, after nearly 30 years, only partly realized. It would seem reasonable, therefore, to anticipate a period of 25 to 50 years in any comprehensive plans for the future, and in doing so they should represent the normal annual development multiplied by 25 or 50 without implying any increase in normal average expenditure.

This much far-sight at least would be required to insure against the destruction in one decade of what has been built in an earlier one while at the same time paving the way to ultimate results not possible in individual projects. The cost of public works is largely a state of mind, and while we are accustomed to the costs of naval vessels and great reclamation works, we are not accustomed to compare the cost of the Capitol on the Hill, symbolizing the whole Nation, with the cost of single units in a naval program, or to the thought that a dozen navies have been built and scrapped while the Capitol has been serving the Nation, and that it stands to-day, as through its whole history, one of the notable buildings of the world.

Turning for a moment to the model of the departmental buildings as exhibited here to-night—the line of buildings facing on B Street and continued west beyond the Monument toward the river—would cost much less than a line of warships of the same length and would outlive them by more than a century. Or, as another example, the cost of the two airplane carriers recently constructed would more than build and equip all of the buildings in the triangle.

A National Capital or a Federal city has stood as a challenge to the American people ever since provision was made for it in the Constitution and since L'Enfant crystallized in a definite form the vision of Washington and his associates of a city belonging to and typifying the whole Nation, independent of any of the States, a plan so farseeing that the early structures, which were planned in harmony with its spirit, although surrounded for years with thoughtless development, maintain their places as dominating elements in the original plan or in any worthy plan conception of to-day, and affirm the judgment of L'Enfant in fitting the proposed city to the topography of the site.

An era of rapid development is the usual explanation of the lack of vision which characterized the development of Washington after the period of the early Republic. The renewed interest in the National Capital which has followed the plan of 1901 indicates, however, that rapid development offers no excuse but rather demands greater vision. The plan of 1901 made it clear that what was envisioned and physically begun by the founders of the Nation was the only basis upon which it can consistently develop into a great and beautiful Capital.

Perhaps it was because there was no complicated group of local city interests to confuse the vision of its founders, and because in their minds there must have been a firm intention that such interests when they came should always be secondary and kept in their true relation to the national character of the city; that the construction of all the early public works was begun with the plans of L'Enfant taken for granted and apparently without the suspicion that they would be forgotten and ignored. It would seem wise for us to think of the Washington of the future as it was thought of by its founders, and in all public works or legislation affecting the city to have in mind the dignity and distinction of its ultimate character as a national city distinguished from the great commercial cities which justly and fittingly express their raison d'être, each in its own way. There should be no conflicting national and local interests; as the Capitol on the Hill is the Nation's Capitol, so the city must always be the Nation's city. It was founded for this purpose, and its construction nobly begun and its future left in faith and trust to the successors of the founders. Washington is the place where it seems to me more than anywhere else all the men who have loved this country and planned great things for it and had visions of its greatness and power live to-day in the life they have put into it.

The costs of building and maintaining a nation's capital have been the subject of much controversy, and it is not my purpose to discuss the merits of the many suggestions which have been offered; but I believe the effect upon the character of the Capital of the application of certain principles demands careful consideration. Washington should not only be the seat of the National Government but should also invite as its guests the national organizations having to do with the arts and sciences and the cultural and spiritual elements of life. If the Capital is to become the cultural center of the Nation, the housing of such interests requires the creation and maintenance of streets and utilities, police and fire protection, and many other obligations of a city government, and it would seem as if a plan could reasonably be devised by which the national and local interests could be definitely segregated, permitting the Capital to be built as generously as it may wish of the love of a whole Nation, without complication with the finances of the District, reaffirming the original hope that Washington should never become a competitor of the commercial and industrial centers of the country.

Frequent reference has been made to the L'Enfant plan, and so much has been said concerning it that it seems important to discuss those elements which make it applicable to the present time and not merely an interesting historic document. Its greatness lies in its simplicity and in its development to the utmost of the topography of the District.

With the Capitol placed upon the hill, a great park extends westward to the river, thus giving the Capitol major importance for all time. The center of this park was planned as an open mall dominated by the dome of the Capitol. From the center of the dome great arterial avenues radiated in all directions, each of which led up to and in turn was dominated by the dome, thus radiating the influence of the Capitol to all parts of the city, and in turn leading all parts of the city up to the Capitol. The same arrangement focused upon the President's house, which also had its own great park, though of lesser importance in the plan, leading southward to the Mall. The intersection of the great diagonal avenues offered minor focal points as ideal locations for memorials of the Nation's history. Lying between these great thoroughfares, a network of smaller streets offered access to individual properties not exposed to the confusion of the heavier traffic on the main arteries. This is a controlling principle sought to-day in all modern planning and zoning regulations.

The flexibility of the L'Enfant plan is best illustrated by the fact that many developments of the present day, undreamed of in L'Enfant's time, find their best expression by conformity with the greater elements of his plan. As a specific illustration, the Department of Commerce, now building, houses one of the greatest activities of the Federal Government and is a structure of such great size that it would be a dominating element in any large city. Every apartment within this building has been designed to meet the requirements of the particular work which will be housed in it. These apartments have been assembled into a great building and take their relative places within it. The building itself, however, becomes merely a unit in a greater project known as the triangle development. The name "Triangle" is merely an acknowledgment of the L'Enfant plan and represents the triangular space lying between Pennsylvania Avenue, radiating from the Capitol toward the northwest, and the boundaries of the Mall, running directly west from the Capitol Grounds. This larger unit in itself recognizes the greater plan and has been designed to create a monumental and effective separation of B Street and Pennsylvania Avenue at the apex of the triangle and to make a fitting closure of the cross vista from the Mall to the Department of Justice Building. It gives a façade to Pennsylvania Avenue worthy of the importance of that thoroughfare and creates on B Street a part of the great frame of the Mall envisioned by L'Enfant, holding the city back from the great central motif in which the Nation's tributes to Washington and Lincoln are enshrined as no other location, however commanding, could enshrine them. Imagine these same two monuments erected anywhere in the built-up part of the city and deprived of their reverent isolation!

By the application of the principle that, no matter how important the project, it must take its place in the treatment of the whole, it has been possible to make every office in the proposed group of departmental buildings not only serve its own purpose in the most efficient way but do its part in paying homage to the great central motif of the city and to the majestic simplicity of the L'Enfant plan. This treatment points the way for the location and design of such buildings as will be needed in the future to the west of the Monument and for the completion of the frame on the south side of the Mall.

At the present time the Mall is marred by the temporary buildings erected during the war. The Munitions and Navy Buildings should be removed and their functions housed on the north side of B Street. They now occupy a site originally planted with trees, and during the 10 years since the war the balancing trees on the south side have grown to such size that it will be many years before a new planting on the north side, on the site of these buildings, can reestablish the balance necessary to the setting of the Lincoln Memorial. President Lincoln's action in completing the dome of the Capitol during the stress of the Civil War is a significant challenge to the continued obstruction of the park leading up to the Capitol by these war structures.

The Smithsonian group should be studied in order that its future constructions from time to time will ultimately give it its true relation to the L'Enfant plan, one of its units, the Freer Gallery, having already been so placed.

Another interesting illustration of the multiplied values resulting from good planning is the proposed development of a municipal group at John Marshall Place. There is no more beautiful example of early republican architecture in the country than the District Courthouse, now somewhat lost in Judiciary Square and seen by the casual visitor only by accident. By the wise choice of a site and the understanding manner of the planning and designing of the proposed structures, this group, without adding anything to the bulk or cost of its buildings, will frame a portion of the north side of Pennsylvania Avenue, will open a splendid vista through to the courthouse, bringing this ancient building directly into the main plan of the city, and create a monumental frontage for the south side of Judiciary Square, while in turn the old courthouse will add its distinction to the municipal group by occupying the end of its principal court, much as the Madeleine is seen when looking from the Place de la Concorde.

It was for these reasons that the McMillan Commission, after an exhaustive study of the problems confronting the city in 1900, determined that no plan of the city could be devised which would insure a nobler future than that prepared by Major L'Enfant in collaboration with Washington and Jefferson. This commission reaffirmed that plan and extended it to meet the many new conditions which had asserted themselves, and modified it only where original opportunities had been permanently lost.

Many of the proposals of the plan of 1901 for park extensions and building locations have not been realized, and some of them are no longer available. Other great assets of the Capital pointed out in that plan are still available, but may not long remain so. I have in mind the development of the great scenic region extending from Potomac Park up to and including the Great Falls of the Potomac. The lower portion of the river is now happily made available by the legislation creating Mount Vernon Boulevard. With a park development extending from this boulevard up to and including the falls, Washington would have a river park unrivaled by any of the world's capitals. The project of the Fort Drive, connecting the ring of Civil War forts occupying the heights around the city, is rapidly becoming almost impossible of realization.

On the other hand, much that was proposed by the report and plan of 1901 has been realized—some of it, notably the railroad situation, in spite of what might have been regarded as insurmountable obstacles. The greatness of the plan for the Mall, in its ultimate simple dignity, appealed to the imagination of the then president of the Pennsylvania Railroad and resulted in clearing the way for a realization of the plan not only in the development of the Mall but in the creation of a great gateway to the city in the form of the Union Station and plaza as now constructed and the development of the land from the station to the Capitol as now authorized.

The extension of the Mall and the location of the Lincoln Memorial represent additions to the original plan of elements unknown at the time of its creation, while the Memorial Bridge, connecting the heart of the city with the memories of the Nation's dead at Arlington, completes the greater central motif of the plan of 1901 now approaching realization. The Grant and Meade memorials in Union Plaza insure the development of the head of the Mall as planned and the removal of the temporary war buildings will make possible the opening of the Mall from the Capitol to the Monument. From the Monument to the Lincoln Memorial the plan has been realized and the Arlington Bridge is well under construction. The Washington Monument gardens remain to be treated as a part of the Mall scheme and of the intersection of the White House axis with that of the Mall. It had been hoped that this might be a project inaugurated in connection with Washington's two hundredth birthday.

B Street north was planned as a great ceremonial street, over which corteges might pass from the dome of the Capitol to the Arlington National Cemetery. This also has been provided for and should be realized in the near future.

The proposal that the gardens of the Mall should include buildings of the museum type has been partly realized by the location of the National Museum and the Freer Gallery.

The proposal that a legislative group should be created around Capitol Square, and an executive group about Lafayette Square has been partly realized in the creation of the Senate and House Office Buildings and the proposed additional House Office Building. The Supreme Court has also been authorized in the location proposed. Rock Creek Park has been enlarged and extended, Potomac Park largely realized, and work on the Anacostia Park begun. All of these projects have taken their places as elements of one great plan and would have lost much of their significance if treated as unrelated units like the Interior Department Building.

The buildings of the early Republic were models of good taste, sound design, and beauty of mass, proportion, and detail. These buildings represented a standard unsurpassed in any of the private or semipublic work throughout the country. Jefferson's interest in architecture is historic and his doctrine of the obligation of the Government to set an example in the arts of design governed the early development of the National Capital and should find expression to-day in all the works of the Federal Government.

In addition to the obligation of the Federal and District Governments, the obligation to maintain an appropriate character of the city extends to owners of private property. In this connection we learn of another of the many examples of President Washington's wisdom and vision. In the original terms governing the building of the Capital he made the design and materials of construction of private structures subject to such regulations as might be thought necessary to insure their appropriateness. Unhappily, this control has long since been relinquished, but it is a matter for congratulation that the legislation recently proposed for reestablishment of such control has received the almost unanimous approval of the citizens of Washington, and it is to be hoped that before long such legislation may be enacted into law.

Our national forests and parks witness our faith that the beauty of woodland and meadow are as necessary to a wholesome national life as their material products. The building of our National Capital should witness the same faith.

In closing, let me again repeat and leave with you the statement that no city can have dignity, beauty, and distinction, or be a great city in the best sense of the word unless its every element is an appropriate part of a greater whole.

The plan of 1901 has never been officially adopted; its intrinsic merit has given it force and carried conviction. Since 1901 the National Commission of Fine Arts has been created, and more recently the National Capital Park and Planning Commission. These two agencies have been governed in their advice and decisions on all individual projects by the relation such projects bear to the city as one great unit.

THE CITY POST OFFICE, WASHINGTON, D. C., IN 1920

(View from North Capitol Street)

Courtesy of the United States Army Air Corps   (View from the Lincoln Memorial)

THE WASHINGTON MONUMENT

Courtesy of the United States Army Air Corps   (View from over Seventeenth Street)

AIRPLANE VIEW OF THE LINCOLN MEMORIAL

AIRPLANE VIEW OF THE NEW NATIONAL MUSEUM

PLAN OF THE MALL, SHOWING EXISTING CONDITIONS IN 1928

This plan shows clearly the temporary war buildings in the Mall and near the Lincoln Memorial which conflict with the execution of the Mall plan as proposed in 1901. These temporary buildings are to be replaced in part by the new structures proposed to be built in the triangle between Pennsylvania Avenue and B Street.

PROCEEDINGS OF APRIL 26, 1929

WASHINGTON, WITH STUDIES FOR FURTHER DEVELOPMENT OF THE MALL

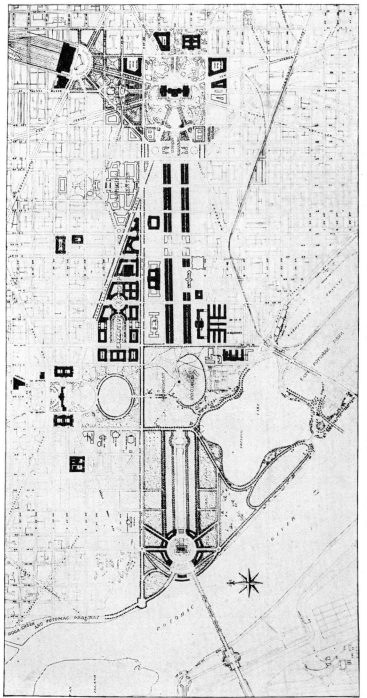

PLAN OF THE MALL, SHOWING THE APPROVED PROJECTS OF 1928

The projects now under way which fit into the general scheme as outlined in 1901 are: 1. The great triangle development for the executive offices; 2. The Capitol Plaza or Union Station Plaza development, between the Union Station and the Capitol; 3. The great avenue of the Mall; 4. The municipal center group between the old city hall, now the Court House, and the Mall; 5. The Arlington Memorial Bridge; 6. Widening and extension of B Street north from the Capitol to the bridge; 7. Connection of Rock Creek and Potomac Parks by a parkway from the Lincoln Memorial.

ORIGIN OF THE PLAN OF 1901

ADDRESS OF

CHARLES MOORE

Chairman of the National Commission of Fine Arts

O-NIGHT the past rises before me as a dream. Last night I listened to the powerful Secretary Mellon take the executive responsibility in formulating and carrying out plans for the greatest group of public buildings ever constructed at one time in the history of the world. Then President Hoover placed behind the project the force of his office and his personality. Senator Smoot and Representative Elliott told of securing the abundant legislation from the Congress inspired by their patriotic appeals. As I listened to these pæans my memory went back over the 27 years to that snowy afternoon of January 15, 1902, when, at the Corcoran Gallery, Senator McMillan, on behalf of the Committee on the District of Columbia, revealed the plan of 1901 to President Roosevelt and his Cabinet, notably to Secretaries John Hay and Elihu Root, all three of whom became its aggressive and effective supporters, and by their official acts drove the firm pegs that fastened that plan for the ages to come.

Through the bewildering fogs of indifference, over the treacherous shoals of misunderstanding, amid the sharp reefs of opposition, the staunch plan of 1901 has been steered into its appointed harbor of realization, there to discharge its cargo of benefits and blessings.

Later in the evening you shall see on the screen the achievements of a quarter century; and also goals for future striving; for so long as the Nation lives its Capital never will be finished. What you will not see depicted are the struggles, often heart breaking struggles, that marked every one of these now lauded triumphs. Those conflicts are now swallowed up in victory.

Time fails me to name the noble host who have come forward in time of peril to do battle for the unity, the dignity, the beauty of the Capital of the United States.

There is fascination in the fray—something akin to the lure of the crusaders to rescue the Holy City from the infidel. It means thought and time and patience and rebuffs and misrepresentation of motives, but it is worth the sacrifice.

It may be only fancy on my part, but I suspect strongly that no future triumphs possible to national finance are so alluring or stimulating or satisfying to Mr. Mellon as is the quest on which he is now embarked—the quest of good order and beauty made incarnate in the National Capital.

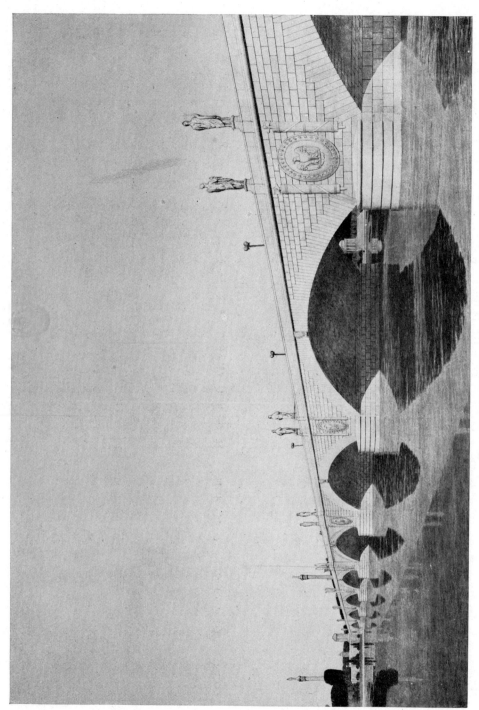

THE ARLINGTON MEMORIAL BRIDGE
(Perspective of completed bridge)

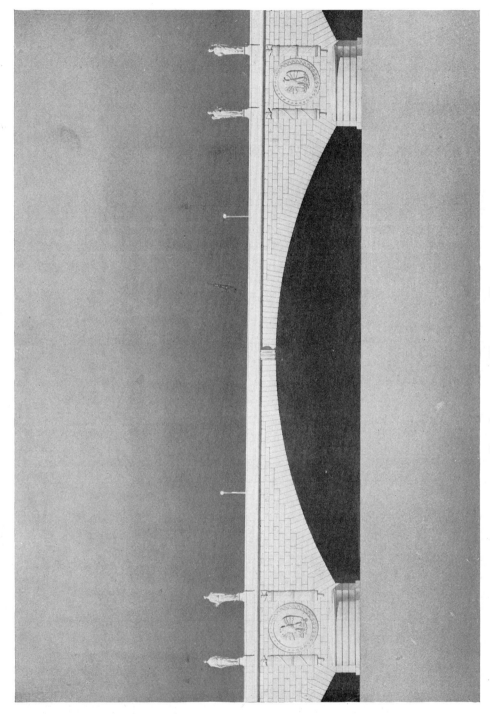

THE ARLINGTON MEMORIAL BRIDGE
(Detail of piers and span)

THE ARLINGTON MEMORIAL BRIDGE
(View during construction)

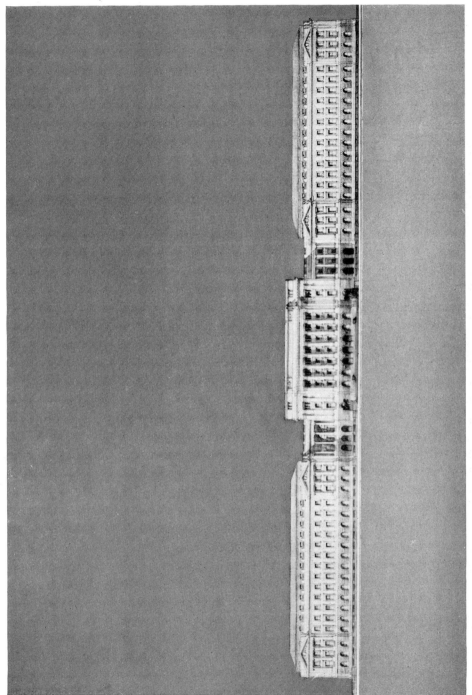

The Department of Agriculture as Completed in 1929

THE TRIANGLE AND THE MALL, SHOWING PROPOSED NEW BUILDINGS

THE ARCHITECTURE OF THE CAPITAL

ADDRESS OF

EDWARD H. BENNETT

Chairman of the Architectural Consultants, Treasury Department

I AM to speak about the development of Washington, with special reference to the areas in which the new departmental and other Government buildings will be placed. This area, roughly speaking, lies between Pennsylvania Avenue and Maryland Avenue, the Capitol, and the Monument. I shall refer most specifically in my remarks to the area now known as the "Triangle," between Pennsylvania Avenue and B Street, and, since this whole subject has been so splendidly covered in the speech of the Secretary of the Treasury recently at Pittsburgh, I shall quote in places from his statement.

It is obvious at the start that this, although an element in the plan of Washington, is a very important one in the composition of its plan, and particularly of the plan of the future Washington. I should like to emphasize at the start the orderly relationship of the plan of this great section of land to that of the whole Mall.

"Congress has made the necessary appropriation to initiate this work and to carry out the most important features of that long-neglected plan of Washington and L'Enfant for the development of the city. The responsibility for carrying out this plan, by the purchase of sites and the erection of buildings, was placed by Congress on the Secretary of the Treasury and has become, therefore, an integral part of Treasury activities."

The present gathering meets in a sense to pay a tribute to order, as I see it, a human order, the product of centuries of civilization as expressed in the thoughts of men and the works of their hands. It is not the order of nature so far as one can see. That we may realize by taking a trip out into the cosmos under the guidance of a great scientist like Jeans, Eddington, or our own Milliken. We encounter nebulæ, galactic clusters, solar systems, myriad masses of suns, and so-called cosmic dust, into the infinite. But spirals, whorls, everywhere! No tangible arrangement as recognized by the cultivated intelligence of the human being.

One returns with a sense of relief to considerations of order as related to the human mind, expressed in its architectural works, and with joy if we can see the beauty of this order and its rhythm. It is an order more nearly related to that natural to the smaller expressions of the creation as evidenced by the structures of crystals, plant life, and animal life, the compositions of which all relate to a simple plan in which there are dominant and subordinate elements.

We are this evening to get a glimpse of the beauty of Washington in its past, present, and future. To do that we must first see and appreciate the underlying system or order of its great plan.

An architectural plan! We may well rejoice that the original plan was made. Suppose, for example, there had been no plan of L'Enfant and General Washington. It might easily have been the case, as has been the fate of most other great capitals early founded, whose plans have been later rectified, and as in the case of Paris, made superb. Most cities have grown from a congerie of huts, evolved more or less according to the necessities of the situation as controlled by the growing intelligence of the inhabitants. But in the case of Washington enough great precedent had been established—a conscious idea of city planning existed in Europe and very distinctly in the early days of the United States.

The orderly mind of the great Washington saw the necessity of planning ahead of the actual needs and he must have seen the possible beauty of a city planned on formal lines—formal, or perhaps more correctly, regular lines. It was essentially a formal age. No doubt life pulsated just as keenly in humanity as to-day, but it seemed more disciplined and, in its social contacts, ordered. Hence the ordered and rhythmic expression of the architecture of the day, and hence, added to the great new outlook in life on a vast continent, the potentiality of which was becoming apparent, the instinctive, if not conscious aim to lay foundations in an orderly and comprehensive manner. Hence, the Washington of the past.

The Washington of the present is the expression of the early plan of 1790, stimulated and corrected by the great plan of the Park Commission of 1901, but as yet incomplete in its execution.

The Washington of the future, based on that which has gone before, must be the result of our efforts of to-day. Let alone, it would end in chaos, as has been demonstrated by some of the attempts ignorantly proposed in violation of the original plan. Given meager support, the final result will be no better than it is to-day, but given great and concentrated attention and enthusiastic support by the Nation through its representatives and that collection of splendid men who are giving their time freely in its interest, officially and unofficially, it will become superb.

That is why to-night we are looking at the plan of Washington, and I hope, with the keenest appreciation of the fact that there was the original plan of the Capital. The perspective we have, the past experience of civilization centering on the original plan, its renewal in the plan of 1901, and to-day substantial expansion of that plan, an expansion which is also a consolidation.

Through all this development there have been great personalities involved. Most of them are known to you in history. It is my personal desire to acknowledge our good fortune in that the work of to-day has received not only the support of our leading Executive but an important part of it has been under the direction of the man who, having had the power to help the realization, had also the vision and desire to do so. I allude, of course, to our great Secretary Mellon.

I hope what I have said will not seem too far afield, because I think it is so important that we should realize that this great group of departmental buildings to which I refer in general outline is so strongly related to the general composition of the plan of Washington. The main axis of the Triangle group is parallel to the Mall, not yet completed, stretching from the Capitol to the Lincoln Memorial. The L'Enfant plan did not have compositions lateral to the Mall, although they might well have been incorporated even in that day, as that would have resembled an arrangement of the great eighteenth century French plans, from which the plan of Washington was really evolved. The main axis of the Triangle plan has this further justification in precedent. It is traversed by a series of great axes in extension of existing streets. All this can be seen on the plans and diagrams in the moving pictures.

Important as is this group of the Triangle, it must be remembered that similar developments, though not so extensive, are proposed for the south side of the Mall, and in order to complete the picture of this great composition, which will slowly be realized, one must include the planning of the Capitol approach from the Union Station, including the new park area to the north of the Capitol and the magnificent approach from the gateway of the city by the Union Station to the head of the Mall. These plans, if carried out, founded as they are on a great and substantial ideal, should measure up to the requirements of the Capital of this great country.

In the speech of Secretary Mellon, he said:

It is intended to carry through, as rapidly as possible, the most pressing needs as regards housing of Government departments and activities. These will include a new and larger building for the increased activities of the Department of Commerce, a Supreme Court building, a building for the Bureau of Internal Revenue, an archives building, a building for the Department of Agriculture, still another for the Department of Labor, and several others besides. One of these buildings, that for the Supreme Court, will be placed on Capitol Hill; but, as regards the others, advantage will be taken of this opportunity to group them together in such a way as to contribute in the greatest measure possible to the beauty of Washington.

The general principle has been established that no large departmental buildings are to be placed in the Mall, as was at first proposed, but that the Mall is to be reserved for park purposes and as a site for buildings of a museumlike character.

Departmental buildings are to be placed along the south side of Pennsylvania Avenue from the Treasury to the Capitol. In addition to facing on Pennsylvania Avenue, these buildings will face also on a grand boulevard, which is to be cut through the city, bordering the Mall and stretching from the Capitol to the new Memorial Bridge on the Potomac near the base of the Lincoln Memorial. It is intended the buildings, while having each a separate and distinctive architectural treatment, shall be of harmonious design and grouped around two large interior courts or plazas somewhat after the arrangement of the Louvre in Paris.

A uniform corner height has been observed, although the architecture is varied. The ground contains 70 acres, and it is upward of 3,000 feet in length on B Street. There are upward of 1,000,000 square feet in the Commerce Building alone. The plazas are actually three in number; that on Twelfth Street, the circular one, being in a sense the pivot of the composition. In it we have proposed a great commemorative column. The vistas will extend from this circular plaza through into the other plazas, and especially into the great plaza, which, in turn, opens through an arched way onto Pennsylvania Avenue and toward the Mall, where it has been suggested shall be placed the National Museum of Art. The vital element binding the entire group is the connection between the two larger plazas. A happy solution adjusted to the scale of both has been found, crowned by a pavilion giving variety to the silhouette of the group.

Again Secretary Mellon said:

It is easy to see what the effect will be. As one proceeds down Pennsylvania Avenue toward the Capitol, on the south side will be a succession of beautiful and harmonious buildings, all of a design in keeping with the semiclassical tradition so well established in Washington. On the north side vistas will be opened up, so that groups of buildings, such as the beautiful District of Columbia Courthouse, on John Marshall Place, shall be brought into the general plan of Pennsylvania Avenue. At the same time the Mall will present the spectacle of a great park bordered on one side by the new boulevard lined with beautiful buildings, a wide parkway of greensward with its four rows of trees, its drives and walks, statues, and reflecting pools, all arranged in such a way that long vistas will be opened up for views of the Capitol in one direction and of the Washington Monument and Lincoln Memorial in the other.

To realize the force of this axial arrangement one must see it after dusk. Sounds of the activities of the city are heard in the distance, but the Mall, with its three great structures—the Capitol, the Monument, and the Lincoln Memorial, aglow and reflected in the pools—is silent and conveys a sense of strength; the strength and confidence of a nation.

(View from Fifteenth Street, looking east)

MODEL OF THE PROPOSED GOVERNMENT BUILDINGS WITHIN THE TRIANGLE BOUNDED BY PENNSYLVANIA AVENUE, FIFTEENTH STREET, AND B STREET

THE TRIANGLE MODEL

(View looking west)

The Triangle Model, Pennsylvania Avenue Front

(View looking east)

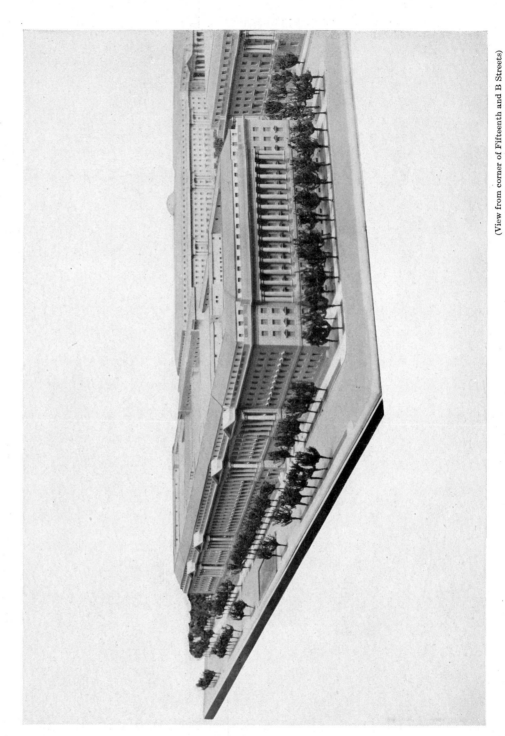

The Triangle Model, Department of Commerce Building

(View from corner of Fifteenth and B Streets)

The Main Court of the Triangle Model

(View from interior park, looking east)

PROPOSED PLAN FOR THE MUNICIPAL CENTER, NORTH SIDE PENNSYLVANIA AVENUE, THIRD TO SIXTH STREETS

THE MUNICIPAL CENTER

ADDRESS OF

LAYSON E. ATKINS

Major, U. S. A., and Assistant Engineer Commissioner of the District of Columbia

HE completion of the municipal center of the city of Washington will give to the world a more adequate expression of Washington as a municipality. As the Federal development of the triangle will express the growth and importance of the Federal Government, so the municipal center will express the dignity and importance of Washington as a city. These two groups of buildings will form a magnificent nucleus for the new and greater Washington of the future. The present District Building, constructed in 1908, has for some time been too small to accommodate the various executive departments of our city government. When this structure was erected it was expected that future expansion would be provided by building an addition on the square to the south of the present building, which would be connected by bridges over D Street. The execution of the plans of the Federal Government for a monumental group of buildings to house the different governmental departments south of Pennsylvania Avenue not only precludes the possibility of constructing this addition but also requires the replacement of the present District Building by a new structure in harmony with the general development of the Federal triangle. Therefore it was necessary for District officials to find a new location on which to erect buildings to properly accommodate the functions of the city government.

A committee was appointed March 12, 1927, to study the situation and to recommend a new location. After a careful study, it was finally decided to locate on both sides of John Marshall Place (Four-and-one-half Street), north of Pennsylvania Avenue, and to provide for practically all departments of the District government in one group of buildings.

Bad as is the need for additional space for the executive departments of the city government, it is even more imperative that provisions be made at once for the police court, the municipal court, the juvenile court, and the recorder of deeds, which are now housed in quarters wholly inadequate and unsuited for their purposes.

The city has in the present District Building a very valuable asset. This should be recognized and credit allowed by the Federal Government in granting the appropriations for the new municipal center. The area of the ground on which the building stands is 46,000 square feet. As a conservative estimate the land is worth $30 per square foot, giving a total value for the land of approximately $1,380,000.

The cost of the present building, when built in 1908, was $1,970,000. In the meantime building costs have more than doubled. If built to-day, the estimated value is about $4,000,000, giving a total value for land and building of $5,300,000. Approximately this sum should be credited to the municipal center by the Federal Government.

The proposed site for the new municipal center faces on the south Pennsylvania Avenue from Third to Sixth Street; on the west Sixth Street; on the north Louisiana Avenue, D Street, and Indiana Avenue; on the east Third Street. This comprises four squares, two on either side of John Marshall Place, which forms the north and south axis of the group. The difference in level between Pennsylvania Avenue and D Street, directly in front of the District Supreme Court Building, is 33 feet. Approximately midway between these two levels will be placed a great court 280 feet in width by 500 feet in length. The approaches to the court from Pennsylvania Avenue will be by a series of steps. Other flights of steps will be placed at the north end from the court level to D Street. The court will be surrounded with an arcade giving direct access to the various parts of the building, offering shelter in inclement weather, and a shady passageway during the hot summer months. The court will be treated as a great garden with trees and flowers and a large pool in the center.

The architecture of the building on Pennsylvania Avenue will harmonize with the Federal buildings on the south side of the Avenue, carrying practically the same belt courses and cornice lines. Due to the difference in elevation of the street, the north front, facing the District Supreme Court Building, will harmonize in scale and style with the architecture of that building.

The District Supreme Court Building, located at the head of John Marshall Place, is one of the most charming and beautiful relics of early Washington. It was designed in 1820 by George Hadfield, an English architect, for use as a city hall. Hadfield came to this country in 1795 to assist Doctor Thornton, who was at that time in charge of the building of the United States Capitol.

The cornerstone of this building was laid August 22, 1820, and it is interesting to note the following from the mayor's proclamation on this occasion:

An edifice devoted to municipal purposes, to be the seat of legislation and of the administration of justice for this metropolis when it will have reached its destined populousness and * * * to be erected on a scale worthy of the uses for which it is intended. * * * Also to be constructed with a view to durability which will extend beyond the age of any of the living, not one of whom will ever witness the recurrence of such an event as the laying of the foundation of this fabric. On behalf of the commissioners appointed to erect this hall I therefore invite you to witness a ceremony so rare in its occurrence that it will be an era in our history, and withal so interesting to all who take an interest in the welfare of the city founded by the departed Washington.

The truth of this prophecy has been borne out, and it is most fitting that our proposed municipal center should have the Supreme Court Building as its central motif. We thus return to the early city hall to develop our plans for a splendid civic center for the future.

The estimated cost of acquiring the four squares in this site is six and one-half million dollars. It is proposed to purchase all of the site at the earliest possible date and to proceed with the erection of a building on the northwest square, bounded by John Marshall Place, C Street, Sixth Street, and Louisiana Avenue, to accommodate the three courts and the recorder of deeds.

What are the advantages of the site selected and the establishment thereon of a group of municipal buildings which will provide accommodations for all of the city's departments?

In my opinion they are as follows:

First. Low cost of land.

The site is located in what is now one of the least-desirable sections of the city, and can be bought at a very reasonable price. There are very few expensive buildings to purchase.

Second. Convenience of location.

The city departments would be conveniently located with reference to the various governmental departments and the Capitol, so that business could be carried on with the maximum of efficiency and ease.

Third. Economy of building costs.

The centralization of the various functions of the District government in one group of buildings tends toward a lower cost of construction than would be possible with the erection of separate buildings at different locations.

Fourth. Economy of administration and operation.

Administration and control would be more direct and efficient in a closely knit organization than in different buildings widely separated. Likewise the operation and maintenance would be less costly and more efficient.

Fifth. Expresses importance of city government.

In a group of important buildings the civic life of the city would be exemplified and the city government, as distinguished from the Federal Government, would find adequate and proper expression.

Sixth. A logical location in harmony with the Federal improvement program.

This location will serve as a dignified and harmonious link between the Federal buildings south of Pennsylvania Avenue, Judiciary Square to the north, and the Capitol Plaza development to the east. It will also be a big step in the development of the proper treatment of the north side of Pennsylvania Avenue.

A bill authorizing the development of these four squares as a municipal center was drafted by the District Commissioners and submitted to the Budget Bureau during the last session of Congress. When transmitted to Congress by the Budget Bureau the bill was changed to cover only two squares. Through the able support of Mr. Underhill and Mr. Simmons in the House of Representatives and of Senator Smoot in the Senate both of these houses amended the bill to authorize the purchase of the full four squares.

Requests for appropriations to purchase the land will be made in our next appropriation act, and it is expected that this splendid group of buildings will begin to take definite form by the erection of the courts building in the near future.

In conclusion, the municipal center will form a vital part in the Federal development of Pennsylvania Avenue and in the beautification of Washington. The city will do its part to carry on the great work begun by Washington, Jefferson, and L'Enfant to establish on the Potomac the most beautiful and impressive Capital City in the world.

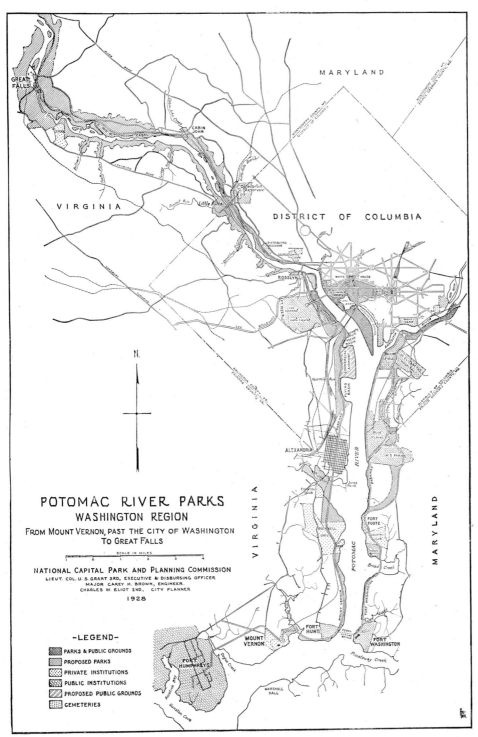

POTOMAC RIVER PARKS
WASHINGTON REGION
From Mount Vernon, Past the City of Washington
To Great Falls

SCALE IN MILES

NATIONAL CAPITAL PARK AND PLANNING COMMISSION
LIEUT. COL. U. S. GRANT 3RD, EXECUTIVE & DISBURSING OFFICER
MAJOR CAREY H. BROWN, ENGINEER.
CHARLES W. ELIOT 2ND, CITY PLANNER

1928

-LEGEND-
PARKS & PUBLIC GROUNDS
PROPOSED PARKS
PRIVATE INSTITUTIONS
PUBLIC INSTITUTIONS
PROPOSED PUBLIC GROUNDS
CEMETERIES

POTOMAC RIVER PARKS, FROM MOUNT VERNON, PAST WASHINGTON TO GREAT FALLS

MODEL OF THE PROPOSED UNITED STATES SUPREME COURT BUILDING

Design for the New Proposed Office Building, United States House of Representatives

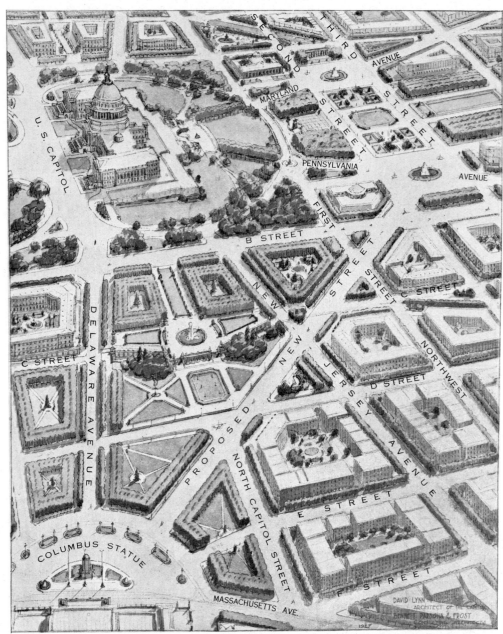

(View looking south from Union Station)

(View looking south from Union Station)

PROPOSED PLAN OF THE ENLARGEMENT OF THE CAPITOL GROUNDS

OUR NATIONAL CAPITAL

ADDRESS OF

LOUIS C. CRAMTON

Member of Congress from Michigan

THE development of the National Capital, to which the Federal Government is now definitely committed, along lines so comprehensive and far-reaching, so in harmony with the plans of Washington and L'Enfant, well deserves to be brought vividly to the knowledge of the Congress, the residents of the Capital City, and the people of the Nation, as our great Secretary of the Treasury is bringing it in this series of meetings. The hope of George Washington, the dream of the Nation, that this Capital City be the most beautiful city in the world, nears realization. But the dream is more than that.

"This is more than the making of a beautiful city," last night said President Hoover in this hall. "Washington is not only the Nation's Capital; it is the symbol of America. By its dignity and architectural inspiration we stimulate pride in our country, we encourage the elevation of thought and character which comes from great architecture." So great an advance in so important a national program deserves to be known and understood of the Nation.

With fortunate and characteristic vision Washington located the new Capital where nature was most charming and gave the great city-to-be a splendid background. Then he brought the young French engineer, Major L'Enfant, to plan with Jefferson and him its development. Now the tomb of L'Enfant, on the brow of Arlington, overlooks all this marvelous fruition of his planning, while his name is imperishable as long as America stands. So wisely did they plan, that through all our history the development of this Capital, now grown from a vision to a city of more than half a million people, is tested by the L'Enfant plan, our great successes in harmony with it, our tragedies of failure when we have departed from it in design or in location.

L'Enfant planned the rectilinear arrangement of streets, with diagonal avenues radiating from Capitol and White House, and with circles at the resultant intersections of more than two thoroughfares. Contributing so much to the beauty of the city, these avenues and circles are of the greatest present-day importance in the handling of a traffic far heavier and far more speedy than any of the horse age could have dreamed of.

NATIONAL CAPITAL IDEA DOMINANT IN THE CITY PLAN

L'Enfant planned for the location of all public buildings in appropriate architectural settings, grouped along a beautiful park, the Mall, connecting Capitol and White House. This being a city created to serve as the National Capital, that purpose is dominant in the L'Enfant plan. It should ever be so in the planning for this Capital City. The city, holding an unrivaled position as the National Capital, never should seek industrial supremacy. To do so would endanger its certain prestige without grasping the industrial mirage. Keeping predominant always the National Capital purpose, this will certainly become a city possessing unrivaled charm and interest, with a minimum of that which would detract.

L'ENFANT PLAN IS REVIVED

The influence of Washington made the L'Enfant plan a reality at once in important respects and then for close to a century its development languished. But upon the celebration of the one hundredth anniversary of the establishment of the seat of government in the District of Columbia, President McKinley brought about a revival of interest in the plan and the McMillan Commission followed. Senator McMillan, of my own State, at that time and for many years, played a highly creditable and influential part in the development of Washington — a part in which the able gentleman who presides to-night, Mr. Charles Moore, shared largely, as he was then at the Senator's side. The resultant plan of 1901 recommended a return to the L'Enfant plan of a century before, with such extension of it as might be required to meet modern conditions and the city's growth. And the L'Enfant plan began again to come into its own.

In 1910 Congress created the Fine Arts Commission and considerably later the Zoning Commission and the National Capital Park and Planning Commission. Nothing is more imperative now from a legislative point of view with reference to the architecture of Washington than the grant of much greater authority to regulate the character, height, use, and location of private structures conspicuously located especially adjacent to, or in the vicinity of, public parks and public buildings of the District or Federal Governments. Why should the Nation plan and create and then permit the individual, through heedlessness or through selfishness or greed, to negative the national effort and conflict with the common good? The national purpose should be really dominant.

ADDRESS OF LOUIS C. CRAMTON

As one looks back one can clearly see a constant acceleration of movement toward the fullest possible realization of the L'Enfant plan since the McMillan report. A great deal has been accomplished in the past score of years. We are now on the threshold of glorious things.

ON THE THRESHOLD OF GLORIOUS THINGS

Measured in money, the figures are quite astounding, even in this day, when the common talk of billions make millions seem commonplace. Much has recently been completed of great importance—the development of East Potomac Park, the Arlington Memorial and Amphitheater, the Lincoln Memorial, are preeminent among numerous great gains now accomplished. We have now under construction or authorized for early construction the following highly important and desirable improvements at the sole expense of the Federal Government, and this list is not at all complete:

Botanical Gardens	$820,000
National Arboretum	300,000
Congressional Library, additional site	600,000
Walter Reed Hospital buildings	1,012,000
New Army air field	1,010,000
Government Printing Office	1,250,000
Restoration Arlington Mansion	160,000
Completion Tomb Unknown Soldier at Arlington	400,000
Arlington Memorial Bridge	14,750,000
Mount Vernon Memorial Highway	4,500,000
Addition House Office Building	8,400,000
Enlargement of Capitol Grounds	6,244,472
Supreme Court site and building	7,500,000
Triangle land	25,000,000
Department of Agriculture buildings	8,100,000
Archives Building	8,700,000
Department of Commerce Building	17,500,000
Internal Revenue Building	10,000,000
Total	116,246,472

$265,000,000 FOR NATIONAL CAPITAL IMPROVEMENTS

That total includes only projects, permanent improvements, many of great interest, now under construction or now authorized, and paid for by the Nation. But it does not include all of the proposed triangle program of Federal buildings, to which program this administration and the Congress are in effect fully committed and for which authorizations and appropriations are very sure to follow as rapidly as construction is feasible. In his address in this hall last night Senator Smoot (and no one is better qualified to speak with authority on this) named $200,000,000 as the amount necessary to complete the present triangle building program. Accepting that figure, and including the full triangle program in my tabulation of expenditures now under way and committed, the total is above $265,000,000. Possibly L'Enfant never dreamed there would be that much money in this Nation; in his day thinly scattered along a seaboard, only six million of them, citizens of several contending and jealous States, jealous of each other, but above all jealous of increase of power in the Federal Government. That people have swept across a continent and beyond, have become a hundred and twenty million, with forty-eight strong and prosperous States, and a respected and trusted Federal Government, which now is spending its money by the hundreds of millions in the improvement and beautification of the National Capital. And while they could not have dreamed our progress, Washington and L'Enfant planned for the expenditure of this money. And it is sometimes suggested that the Federal Government lacks in generosity in expenditures for the improvement of the Capital City.

VISUALIZE THE PENDING CHANGES

We are on the threshold of glorious things, we are in the midst of their accomplishment. The realization of them should, indeed, stimulate our pride of country, stimulate and elevate our thought. Let us visualize the physical change in the city. South of the Capitol a new unit will match the present House Office Building, to the east the new Supreme Court building will rise, adjacent to the Congressional Library. To the north the Capitol Grounds will extend to the Columbus Memorial and the Union Station. A boulevard will extend from the Union Station to B Street NW. and along B Street to the Arlington Memorial Bridge, and on to Arlington or to Mount Vernon. This boulevard and the new municipal center to be erected by the District government will clear away from the north side of Pennsylvania Avenue from the Capitol to Sixth Street the cheap lodging houses, the questionable resorts, the Chinese emporium, and the tattooing places which now give that conspicuous area a character of its own, better to be remembered than endured.

The Union Square and the Mall come into their own; the Grant Memorial may be better appreciated; the Botanical Garden is removed and will blossom more gloriously elsewhere; the World War temporary shacks, which have so long outstayed their welcome, will vanish; the Agricultural Building steps back to the proper alignment and becomes an architectural asset instead of a liability. For the north boundary of the Mall the L'Enfant vision of stately public buildings properly landscaped will succeed the present strange mixture of the useful and the tolerated in commercial architecture which now reduce this heart center of the Capital to the level of hundreds of other cities properly unsung. From the White House to the Capitol, the south side of historic Pennsylvania Avenue, where have traveled these many years great democracy's chosen leaders and loved heroes, will be the imposing Federal buildings of the Triangle program, not competing with each other and swearing at each other in varying forms of architecture, but each contributing to a beautiful whole that will add something to the world's architecture. As L'Enfant and Washington would have it, the Capital City will then present to the world a clean face with beautiful features, and gone will be all the marks of tattooing, the stains of chop suey, and the plague of room-rent signs.

PRESERVATION OF NATURE'S CHARMS MUST ACCOMPANY MAN'S IMPROVEMENTS

There are thousands of our citizens, remote from the Capital, hoping not at all that they may ever see its beauties in the real but echoing in their hearts the same desire that President Coolidge expressed in his last annual message to Congress when he said: "If our country wishes to compete with others, let it not be in the support of armaments but in the making of a beautiful Capital City. Let it express the soul of America."

They want it to be the most beautiful city, combining in perfection the man-made wonders with the natural charms which came from the Creator. It must not be all a man-made city, for as such it rises not to its highest level.

Washington located the new Capital in the midst of lavish display of beauties of God's handiwork. At the head of navigation of the great Potomac, in the midst of wooded hills, its many valleys carrying creeks that enliven the landscape. While we make a reality of the dreams of L'Enfant in carrying forward man-made beauties, we must not permit the beautiful scenic realities of Washington's time to become only mourned memories. Washington must have loved the Potomac as it flowed past his home and his great estate, must have been thrilled by Great Falls, where he went so often, must have loved the hills and streams surrounding the site he chose for his country's Capital, or he would not have so chosen. Just as he inspired the L'Enfant plan of development we now promote, he would have preserved those beauties.

It is wonderful we are proceeding now so rapidly and so wisely with our architectural development, but delay in this has not been fatal. What was not done fifty years ago may be done now, and the error of fifty years ago may now be corrected. I like to cherish the hope that even the highly individualistic State, War, and Navy Departments Building may yet come out of its architectural cocoon and take on a beauty of exterior that will harmonize with the beauty of its neighbors.

That which man made man may replace and when he will. But the beauties of nature man can not restore when once destroyed. Those woods which Washington loved are disappearing; those charming ravines are being leveled; those splendid palisades of the Potomac are daily scenes of blasting that rob them of primeval beauty.

The preservation of all this has had much of thought by our leaders, has been the subject of wise planning, but the plans have been disastrously slow in realization. The beauty is passing and can not be restored.

DISASTROUS DELAY IN PARK AND PLAYGROUNDS PLAN

Through the legislation of 1924 and 1926 the National Capital Park and Planning Commission came into being with remarkably able personnel, all characterized by high zeal and great ability. Two years ago they completed a plan of lands in the District and its environs which should be purchased for park, parkway, and playground purposes of the National Capital, this program being estimated then to cost $15,750,000 if promptly carried out. Under the act creating the commission the cost of such purchases is to be borne as other expenses of the District, the Federal Government contributing a lump sum or a percentage, as the case may be. As $6,000,000 of the amount named is for playgrounds, and the other areas are of great traffic use or recreational use to the people of the District, and as the Federal Government has under way the expenditure of over $265,000,000, that act of Congress was not unfair as to lands in the District. But under that authority only $600,000 to $1,000,000 has been spent annually for such purchases. Those lands are increasing in value at least 10 per cent per year. Will some Einstein tell us, if the Planning Commission program goes up in cost $1,500,000 a year and they can only spend $1,000,000, as will be the case next year, how long will it take to buy the lands they want? And in the meantime the ax, the steam shovel, the dynamite are destroying much that Washington would have preserved and no one can restore.

In the report of the Senate District Committee on the bill to create the commission that committee declared a very urgent need to be the establishment of the "Fort Boulevard following the hills encircling the city and connecting the Civil War forts," many of which are still well preserved. The development of the city makes this now difficult. If action is not soon taken, it will be impossible. Encroachment on the sources of the Rock Creek in Maryland threatens the very existence of that stream, the golden thread that binds together the beauty of our greatest park. The valleys tributary of Rock Creek, the Anacostia, the Potomac, the very Palisades, are in process of destruction or are in peril.

ADDRESS OF LOUIS C. CRAMTON

LEGISLATION PENDING WOULD SAVE SCENIC CHARMS

With gratifying unanimity the people of the District, as well as of the Nation, are indorsing legislation now pending which proposes to relieve the District from share in such purchases outside the District and to advance from the Federal Treasury for such purchases money without interest sufficient for the prompt purchase of all the needed lands. Passage of this legislation will insure proper playground development in the District for our children, instead of waiting for their grandchildren, will save $30,000,000, will preserve the scenic beauties of the Capital and its environs. It will give us the George Washington memorial parkway, controlling both banks of the Potomac from Mount Vernon to Great Falls. That legislation is the next step needed in congressional authorization, and it is not to be doubted it soon will follow.

Land taken for public use under a wise policy of park and playground expansion does not injuriously affect the assessment rolls by its removal from taxation. Assessor Richards recently stated in House hearings that increased valuations adjacent would equalize the situation and that the money paid for such lands would seldom leave the District but would instead be used in desirable development elsewhere in the District. For instance, the money the Government paid for the square on which was built the Senate Office Building was used to develop six squares of desirable residences in Mount Pleasant.

A GLORIOUS FUTURE THROUGH FAITHFULNESS TO THE IDEALS OF THE FATHERS

It is fine that as the Nation has grown stronger in numbers, in territory, in prestige, in influence, we still draw our inspiration from the founders. It is eloquent tribute to their kindred wisdom and common Americanism that Coolidge, Hoover, and Mellon carry on in the realization of the dreams and plans of Washington, Jefferson, and L'Enfant—that we prepare for a more glorious future through our faithfulness to the ideals of the fathers.

AIRPLANE VIEW OF THE POTOMAC RIVER FROM OVER GREAT FALLS

(Looking east)

AIRPLANE VIEW OF THE ARLINGTON AMPHITHEATER AND THE TOMB OF THE UNKNOWN SOLDIER

AIRPLANE VIEW OF MOUNT VERNON FROM OVER THE POTOMAC RIVER

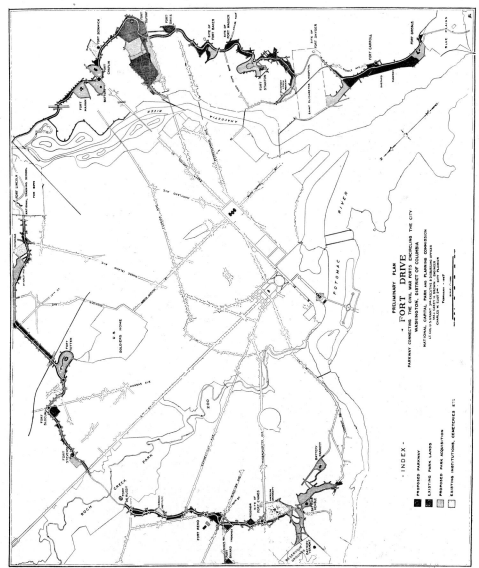

FORT DRIVE CONNECTING THE CIVIL WAR FORTS ENCIRCLING WASHINGTON

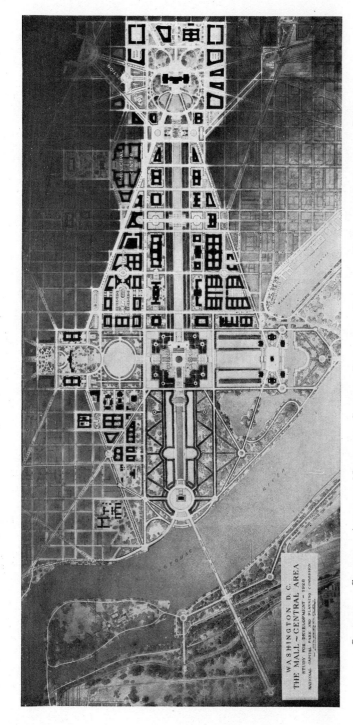

STUDY OF CENTRAL AREA BY NATIONAL CAPITAL PARK AND PLANNING COMMISSION, SHOWING PROJECTS
APPROVED IN 1928 AND POSSIBLE ULTIMATE DEVELOPMENT